On a car journey in France

i-spy

INTRODUCTION

The populations of France and the United Kingdom are similar but in terms of land area, France is more than twice as big. By British standards, therefore, France is a very rural country. And, once you are out of the larger towns and cities, this is the impression you have as you drive along kilometre after kilometre of arrow-straight, tree-lined roads bordered by hectares of maize or sunflowers. Bordered by three seas – the English Channel, the Atlantic Ocean and the Mediterranean Sea – France is a country of variety, and, at the same time, one of strong national identity. As a nation, France is proud of its language, its culture, and its heritage, and its people remain as individual as any in the world. For these reasons, any visitor to the country will instantly recognize its Frenchness but, at the same time, the variety and individuality provide an ideal opportunity for i-SPY.

In the south, the French Riviera is a region of golden beaches where the rich and famous bask under the hot Mediterranean sun. In the north, in Normandy, where a more 'English' climate prevails, dairy farming and apple orchards abound. There are the mountains of the Auvergne and the Massif Central; to the south, France and Spain are separated by the mighty Pyrenees; and to the southeast the Alps provide a spectacular divide between France and Switzerland.

Prehistoric caves, Roman ruins, medieval towns with cobbled streets, châteaux large and small, and the most romantic and stylish of cities, Paris, all contrive to add interest to a land rich in elegance and beauty. As well as the delights of its landscape and the uniqueness of its people, there are two more features of France that serve indelibly to identify the country: its cuisine and its wines. Both have been exported to the furthest-flung outposts of the world. But both continue to play a vital role in the everyday life of France and the French. With so many places to visit and so much of interest to see, i-SPY On a Car Journey in France offers a tempting taste of the country's wealth of fascinating features.

How to use your i-SPY book

You need 1000 points to send off for your i-SPY certificate (see page 64) but that is not too difficult because there are masses of points in every book. Each entry has a star or circle and points value beside it. The stars represent harder to spot entries. As you make each i-SPY, write your score in the circle or star.

One of the first things a visitor to France will notice is the variety of French road signs. In many ways, apart from the language differences, the road signs are similar to British signs. In Britain, many drivers use road numbers to navigate from one place to another. French drivers, however, prefer to use place names as a guide, and, in many cases, major place names beyond the driver's destination are used for navigation.

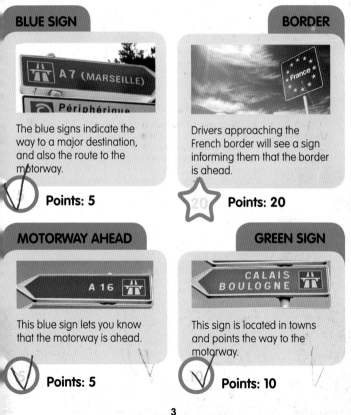

BLUE SIGN

The blue signs indicate the way to a major destination, and also the route to the motorway.

Points: 5

BORDER

Drivers approaching the French border will see a sign informing them that the border is ahead.

Points: 20

MOTORWAY AHEAD

This blue sign lets you know that the motorway is ahead.

Points: 5

GREEN SIGN

This sign is located in towns and points the way to the motorway.

Points: 10

MOTORWAY

If you see one of these, you are now on the motorway!

✓ **Points: 5**

MULTIPLE SIGNS

A 10 E5
BORDEAUX

A 83
NANTES

2000 m

Here is a sign with multiple destinations and route options.

✓ **Points: 10**

WEATHER RESTRICTOR

The speed limit on French motorways varies depending on weather conditions:
130 km/h in good weather,
110 km/h when it is raining.

✓ **Points: 10**

PÉAGE

A road toll is required when travelling on some major French roads. Vehicles are shown here making their payment at a péage station.

Points: 10

EXIT

Exit ahead!

Points: 5

END OF THE MOTORWAY

You have reached the end of the motorway.

Points: 10

ONE WAY

Points: 5

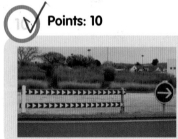

An arrow indicates the direction of flow.

Points: 10

CHEVRON ARROWS

You will see these arrows on a bend or roundabout.

ROUNDABOUT

Points: 5

Roundabouts mainly operate the same way in France as in Britain – except you must go around anticlockwise!

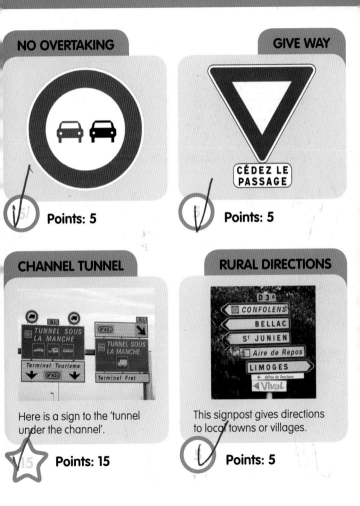

NO OVERTAKING

Points: 5

GIVE WAY

CÉDEZ LE PASSAGE

Points: 5

CHANNEL TUNNEL

Here is a sign to the 'tunnel under the channel'.

Points: 15

RURAL DIRECTIONS

This signpost gives directions to local towns or villages.

Points: 5

NO ENTRY

SAUF CYCLES

Points: 5

ROUNDABOUT

VOUS N'AVEZ PAS LA PRIORITÉ

Approaching a roundabout, you must give way to the traffic already on the roundabout.

Points: 5

NO LEFT TURN

Points: 5

NO RIGHT TURN

Points: 5

STOP

This English word is universally known!

Points: 5

NO WAITING

Points: 5

NO U-TURN

Points: 5

SCHOOL AHEAD

ECOLE

Points: 5

Here are some other road signs you may see.

GRADIENT DOWNHILL

Points: 5

PEDESTRIAN CROSSING

Points: 5

HEIGHT RESTRICTION

3,5 m

Points: 5

TRAFFIC PRIORITY

Points: 5

Just like in Britain, France has various speed limits which must be obeyed. Here are a few to spot. Remember they are in kilometres per hour.

70 KM/H

Points: 5

90 KM/H

Points: 5

110 KM/H

Points: 5

END OF LIMIT

FIN DE ZONE

30

Points: 5

ROAD REPAIR

Points: 20

ROADWORKS

Points: 10

CROSS TO OTHER SIDE

PIÉTONS PASSER EN FACE

Points: 10

ROAD CLOSED

RUE BARRÉE

Points: 10

As you enter a French town, there are always signs to help you.

TOURIST ATTRACTION

This sign indicates that the village has a tourist attraction.

Points: 15

TWINNING

This town is twinned with places in the United Kingdom and Germany.

Points: 15

ENTERING A TOWN

This is the sign you will see on entering a town or village…

Points: 10

LEAVING A TOWN

…and this one when you are leaving it.

Points: 10

LEVEL CROSSING – GUARDED

LEVEL CROSSING – MULTIPLE TRACKS

Points: 10

Points: 20
double if you see a train

15

TAXI RANK

If you need a taxi, it is best to go to a taxi rank outside the train station or a hotel.

Points: 10

PARKING

Motorcycles and bicycles need somewhere to park too!

Points: 10

SPACE INDICATOR

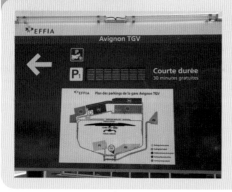

Points: 10

As you approach a town or city, it's a good idea to find out where the car parking spaces are. These signs are a good way to find a space.

Points: 10
for each flag, 5 points for other flags

40 G 5

These can be found outside hôtels de ville and other public buildings.

EUROPEAN UNION

FRANCE

ITALY

UNITED KINGDOM

LEARNER DRIVER

Points: 15

This auto-école roof attachment warns other road users that the car belongs to a driving school and is probably being driven by a learner driver.

Points: 15

PROVISIONAL DRIVER

The 'A' sign in the window indicates that this is a newly-qualified driver.

CITROËN H VAN

Top Spot! Points: 35

This old type of van used to be very popular. They are much harder to find on the roads these days.

CITROËN TRACTION AVANT

Top Spot!   Points: 40

Arno van Dulmen / Shutterstock.com

This Citroën is a symbol of an earlier France. At the time, it was revolutionary as the first mass-produced front-wheel drive car.

CITROËN 2CV

A symbol of France, the Citroën 2CV or Deux-Chevaux is still extremely well-loved, even though they are no longer manufactured.

Points: 10

CITROËN DS

The Citroën DS is another French classic car.

Points: 20

2CV VAN

This 2CV is a multipurpose van…

Points: 15

HAND-PAINTED 2CV

…and this one has been hand-painted! 2CV means 'two horses'.

Points: 25

As France is a rural country, with vast areas of farmland, many animals can be found all over the countryside.

PIG

 Points: 10

COCKEREL

Points: 10

HORSE

Points: 10

SHEEP

 Points: 10

DUCKS

 Points: 5

GOAT

Points: 10

COW

Points: 10

HAY BALE

 Points: 10

In the summer months, the French countryside comes alive with colour. Here are some examples of what you may see.

GRAPES

Points: 15

VINEYARD

Points: 15

SUNFLOWERS

Points: 10

POPPIES

Points: 10

23

Camping is very popular in France and many people spend their holidays on one of the numerous campsites around the country.

CONVERTED VAN

Top Spot! **Points: 40**

This old Citroën H van has been lovingly restored and converted into a camper van.

TENT

An easy way to earn some points on a campsite!

 Points: 5

CARAVAN

A more comfortable way to camp – take your home on wheels with you!

 **Points: 10**

BEWARE OF CYCLISTS

Points: 15

GREEN ROUTE

This route is designated for cyclists and walkers.

Points: 15

CYCLEWAY

This road sign indicates a cyclepath.

Points: 15

HIRE BIKES

Like London, Paris has introduced a successful bikes-for-hire system. It is a great way to see Paris.

Points: 10

Here are a selection of shops that you may find in France. France is famous for its excellent selection of home-grown produce.

BUTCHER

Points: 10

FLORIST

Points: 10

FRUIT AND VEGETABLE STALL

Points: 10

FISHMONGER

Points: 15

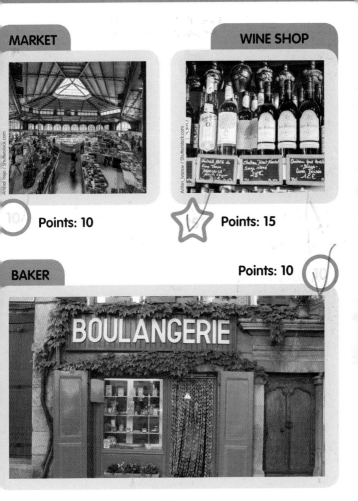

MARKET

Points: 10

WINE SHOP

Points: 15

BAKER

Points: 10

27

PÂTISSERIE

Points: 20
double if you try a macaron

France has many regional banks but you will find branches of these national banks all over the country.

CRÉDIT AGRICOLE

Points: 10

SOCIÉTÉ GÉNÉRALE

Points: 10

CRÉDIT MUTUEL

Points: 10

BNP PARIBAS

Points: 10

TRAIN STATION

Most towns have a train station. This is a picture of the Eurostar station at Lille.

Points: 10
for a train station, double for one with Eurostar

MÉTRO

It is not only Paris that operates an underground or metro railway system. Other French cities have them too. This is Marseille.

Points: 25
double for a non-Paris métro

TRAIN STATION SIGN

Bikeworldtravel / Shutterstock.com

This is a platform sign at a Paris station.

Points: 10

INFORMATION BOOTH

You may need to ask for help or information regarding your journey.

Points: 15

Here are some of the trains that you may find during your travels in France.

Points: 15

LOCAL TRAIN

Local commuter trains often have an upper deck, like a double-decker bus, on their busy routes.

TGV

Points: 20

This is the most prestigious train in France, the TGV, which stands for Train à Grande Vitesse (high-speed train). It can travel over 300 km/h (186 mph).

Points: ~~15~~ 30
double if you travelled in one

EUROSTAR

The Eurostar connects London with stations in Belgium and France, via the Channel Tunnel. You may have started your journey on one!

Situated along the River Seine, Paris is the capital of the republic in every sense. Though, geographically, the city is located towards the north of France, it maintains its status as the physical hub of the country in that the major transport routes radiate outwards like the spokes of a wheel.

EIFFEL TOWER

The Eiffel Tower, built 'temporarily' for the Paris exhibition in 1889, reaches a height of 300 m (984 ft) and fortunately it still stands today.

 Points: 5

GUSTAVE EIFFEL

At the foot of one of the tower's legs is a bust of the Eiffel Tower's builder, the engineer and designer Alexandre Gustave Eiffel (1832–1923).

Points: 15

Points: 10

THE LOUVRE

Famous for da Vinci's priceless Mona Lisa, with her enigmatic smile, the Louvre houses France's most famous art collection.

LOUVRE PYRAMID

Points: 10

France is renowned for its adventurous and avant-garde architecture. Beside the Louvre is a pyramid in glass, surrounded by water spouts, which thrust from the concrete to give access to the gallery beneath.

10 **Points: 10**

ARC DE TRIOMPHE

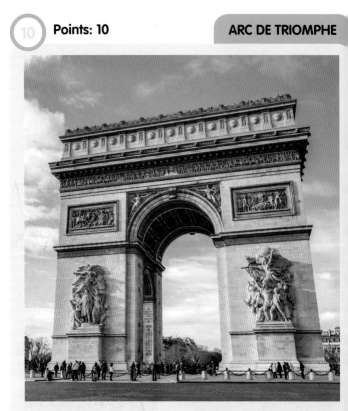

At the end of the Champs-Élysées stands the magnificent Arc de Triomphe built in 1836 to commemorate Napoleon's victories. Beneath the arch is the eternal flame marking the site where an unknown soldier from World War I was buried in 1920.

NOTRE-DAME

Points: 10 10

Cathédrale Notre-Dame, built during the twelfth and thirteenth centuries, was restored during the 1800s and made famous by Victor Hugo's 1831 novel *The Hunchback of Notre-Dame*.

15 **Points: 15**

MONTMARTRE

Kiev Victor / Shutterstock.com

The prominent hill of Montmartre also gives its name to the surrounding district. It is a favourite haunt of painters, sculptors, and musicians, who gather on the famous square, La Place du Tertre.

SACRÉ-COEUR

Points: 15 15

Built in 1876 at the summit of Montmartre, Sacré-Coeur Basilica marks the site where a popular uprising was bloodily repressed in 1871.

MOULIN ROUGE

Points: 15

Opened in 1889 as a cabaret club, the Moulin Rouge was home to the famous cancan dance. Its name means 'Red Mill'.

Points: 15

POMPIDOU CENTRE

Centre Georges Pompidou, known also as Beaubourg, is another centre for the arts. Pompidou (1911–74) was a French statesman and patron of the arts who succeeded de Gaulle as President of the Republic in 1969.

STREET ENTERTAINERS

Points: 10

Outside the Pompidou Centre there is usually a myriad of often-colourful street entertainers.

Points: 15

BATEAUX-MOUCHES

These boats take visitors on a trip along the River Seine, and are a wonderful way to enjoy many of the city sights.

MÉTRO

Points: 5

These elaborate entrances to the Paris Métro – the underground railway – were designed by Hector Guimard (1867-1942), the French Art Nouveau architect.

Points: 15

LES INVALIDES

Today, Les Invalides holds the tombs of France's military heroes, including Napoleon I and Foch, as well as the Musée de l'Armée. It was originally built by Louis XIV as a home for disabled soldiers and has a gold-leafed dome.

POST BOX

The familiar yellow post box of France.

Points: 5

POST BIKE

You may have to be up early in the morning to spot one!

Points: 15

POST OFFICE

La Poste is the national postal service of France.

Points: 5

POST VAN

In its yellow and blue livery, a modern La Poste van is unmistakable.

Points: 10

BUSKER

Points: 15
for each busker playing
a different instrument

There are often several buskers entertaining passers-by in towns and villages.

TOURIST INFORMATION

A tourist information office.

Points: 10

HÔTEL DE VILLE

Not the local hotel, as you might think, but the town hall.

Points: 10

TOWN HALL (MODERN)

Not all hôtels de ville are old, ornate buildings. Here is a modern one in the town centre.

Points: 15

TOWN PLAN

Many towns have detailed maps identifying sites and amenities.

Points: 15

40

Points: 30 Top Spot!

ELECTRIC CAR

Electric cars are becoming more popular in France. Here is one being charged.

FIRE HYDRANT

A modern fire hydrant.

Points: 15

WATER PUMP

This old pump would once have been the only source of fresh drinking water for the locals.

Points: 25

41

BOULES

Points: 15

Pétanque, or boules, is a game played throughout France on almost any piece of spare land. There are regional differences in the way the game is played.

STATUE

This is a statue of Joan of Arc, the Maid of Orléans (1412–1431).

Points: 15
for any equestrian statue

STATUE

Pawel Szczepanski / Shutterstock.com

This is a statue of François Mitterrand, former President of France.

Points: 15
for a statue of any French individual

WAR MEMORIAL

There are many war memorials around France.

Points: 10

WAR GRAVES

The fields of northern France were the site of many battles during both World War I and II. There are thousands of war graves commemorating the fallen soldiers of many different countries.

Points: 15

HOTEL

A large modern hotel in a city centre.

Points: 10

BUDGET HOTEL

A convenient and budget-priced roadside hotel, very popular in France.

Points: 10

UNIVERSITY

Points: 10

France has many universities and colleges. The Sorbonne is in Paris and is one of the most famous universities in the country.

Points: 15
double if you go on a cellar tour

CHAMPAGNE TOUR

Champagne can only be made in a certain area in the northeast region of France. There are some very famous champagne makers and you can go on a tour of their cellars.

Here are some places of entertainment that you may see, or visit.

THEATRE

Frederic Legrand - COMEO / Shutterstock.com

Points: 10

CINEMA

Points: 10

MUSEUM

Points: 10

Taking a canal boat holiday can be a great way of relaxing and seeing the countryside.

CANAL BOAT

Points: 10

Pleasure boating on a canal.

Points: 10

LOCK

Travelling through a lock is all part of the fun of a boating holiday.

RIVER

Points: 10
double if you also see an angler

Angling is as popular a pastime in France as it is in Britain.

Points: 25

CHÂTEAU WITH MOAT

To add an additional line of defence, some châteaux have protective moats around them. The Château of Sully-sur-Loire is located in the Loire Valley. It dates from the 14th century and is a prime example of a medieval fortress.

CHÂTEAU

Points: 10

This is a privately-owned château. The word château can mean castle, fortress, country seat, mansion, hall or palace.

CATHEDRAL

You can find a cathedral in most French cities.

 **Points: 10**

VILLAGE CHURCH

As you travel through France, you will find that most villages, no matter how small, have their own churches.

 **Points: 10**

Points: 20

VIADUCT

Viaducts are long bridges that carry roads or railways over valleys. Many are supported by a series of stone arches, while others are made of metal.

WINDMILL

Points: 15

Windmills use the breeze to turn their sails.This generates power, which has been traditionally used to mill grain or pump water.

Points: 15

WIND TURBINE

Like modern-day windmills, wind turbines use the wind to generate electricity.

WALLED CITY

Points: 25

There would have been many walled cities in medieval France. A handful still exist, their remaining walls creating an imposing barrier.

Points: 25

ARCHAEOLOGICAL SITE

There are many important archaeological sites all over France, many dating back to Roman times.

In France, the law is enforced by both the police, whose vehicles are easily identifiable by red stripes and blue lettering on a white background, and by gendarmes, who drive blue vehicles.

Points: 10

POLICE PATROL CAR

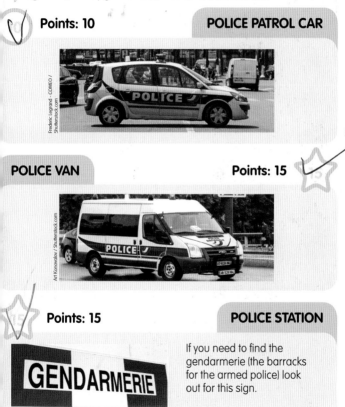

Frederic Legrand - COMEO / Shutterstock.com

POLICE VAN

Points: 15

Art Konovalov / Shutterstock.com

Points: 15

POLICE STATION

If you need to find the gendarmerie (the barracks for the armed police) look out for this sign.

GENDARMERIE

FIRE ENGINE

Points: 15

France's firefighters are known as the sapeurs-pompiers.

Points: 15

AMBULANCE

In case of serious illness or injury, call one of the ambulance services.

POLICE MOTORCYCLE

Points: 15

For rapid response, the police use high-powered motorcycles.

CLIFFS

Points: 20

Northern France lies on the same lines of geology as southern Britain so it's no surprise that long sections of the French coast have rocky cliffs like those in Britain.

Points: 15

Many ports, especially those in the south of France, have glamorous harbours complete with stunning sailing vessels.

Points: 15

The lights warn sailors of dangers, such as rocks. Once, most lighthouses were manned by men who had to make sure everything was in working order and that the lights were lit when necessary. Now they are automated.

Points: 15

SANDY BEACH

France has some wonderful sandy beaches, which are a great holiday attraction for people from many different countries.

BEACH UMBRELLA

Points: 15

It can get very hot at the beach, especially in the south of France, and any shade is often at a premium.

Points: 15

TELESCOPE

You'll often find these telescopes at the seaside. You put a coin in the slot and the telescope works until your time runs out.

PONT DU NORMANDIE

Points: 25

This is one of the longest cable-stayed bridges in the world and is located close to Le Havre. Its total length is 2143 m (7032 ft).

Points: 30   Top Spot!

LE VIADUC DE MILLAU

Another cable-stayed road bridge, the Millau Viaduct is the tallest bridge in the world – the summit of one of the masts is 343 m (1125 ft). It was opened in 2004.

PONT SAINT-BÉNÉZET

Points: 25

Also known as the Pont d'Avignon, this medieval bridge was built between 1171 and 1185. Most of it was swept away in a huge flood in 1668. Only four of the original 22 arches survive.

Points: 20

HOT-AIR BALLOON

Hot-air balloons can often be seen hovering over the countryside on warm days.

POWER STATION

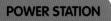

Points: 20

Giant concrete cooling towers puff out clouds of steam from power stations.

OAK

Oak trees provide very strong timbers and are traditionally used in shipbuilding.

 Points: 10

PLANE TREE

Narrow country roads are often lined with plane trees.

Points: 10

POPLAR

Poplar trees are often planted in rows along roadsides in France.

 **Points: 10**

FIR TREE

Tall fir trees are often found in woods and forests.

Points: 10

WEEPING WILLOW

Native to China, the weeping willow can survive almost anywhere, growing best in moist environments.

 Points: 15

CHERRY TREE

Cherry trees have been recorded in France since the Bronze Age period.

Points: 15

SILVER BIRCH

Silver birch is associated with the start of new life due to its ability to colonise bare land after a forest is felled.

 Points: 15

OLIVE TREE

Olive trees were introduced to France 2500 years ago. You'll find them mostly in Provence and the south of France.

Points: 15

PIGEON

Just as in Britain, you will find pigeons flocking in town and city centres.

 Points: 5

MAGPIE

A large black-and-white bird with a long tail. You will often see them feeding on roadkill.

Points: 10

CROW

The small mountain crow, the alpine chough, is found in the high peaks of the Alps, Pyrenees and in the Corsica mountains.

Points: 20

SPARROW

These can be seen dust bathing at the side of the road or scavenging for crumbs at cafés and in town centres.

Points: 10

BLACKBIRD

The male blackbird has shiny black plumage, a yellow beak and a yellow ring around his eye; the female is a dull brown colour.

Points: 10

COMMON GULL

You will see gulls abundant in all coastal regions.

Points: 5

DUCK

There are many breeds of duck found throughout France.

Points: 10

HUMMINGBIRD

Known as sphinx colibri, these stunning little creatures, found in the south of France, are actually moths!

Points: 35 Top Spot!

Even through you have travelled to a different country, there is plenty of evidence of the British at work in France. Here are just a few examples.

HSBC BANK

Points: 15
and for any other familiar shops
or names you find in France!

Points: 15
and for any other familiar shops
or names you find in France!

BARCLAYS BANK

Points: 15
and for any other familiar shops
or names you find in France!

THOMAS COOK

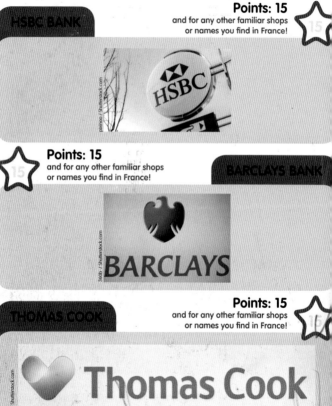

INDEX

i-SPY

How to get your i-SPY certificate and badge

Let us know when you've become a super-spotter with 1000 points and we'll send you a special certificate and badge!

HERE'S WHAT TO DO!

110

- ✓ Ask an adult to check your score.

- ✓ Visit www.collins.co.uk/i-SPY to apply for your certificate. If you are under the age of 13 you will need a parent or guardian to do this.

- ✓ We'll send your certificate via email and you'll receive a brilliant badge through the post!